1945
THE ALLIES VICTORIOUS

1945

THE ALLIES VICTORIOUS

Ross Burns

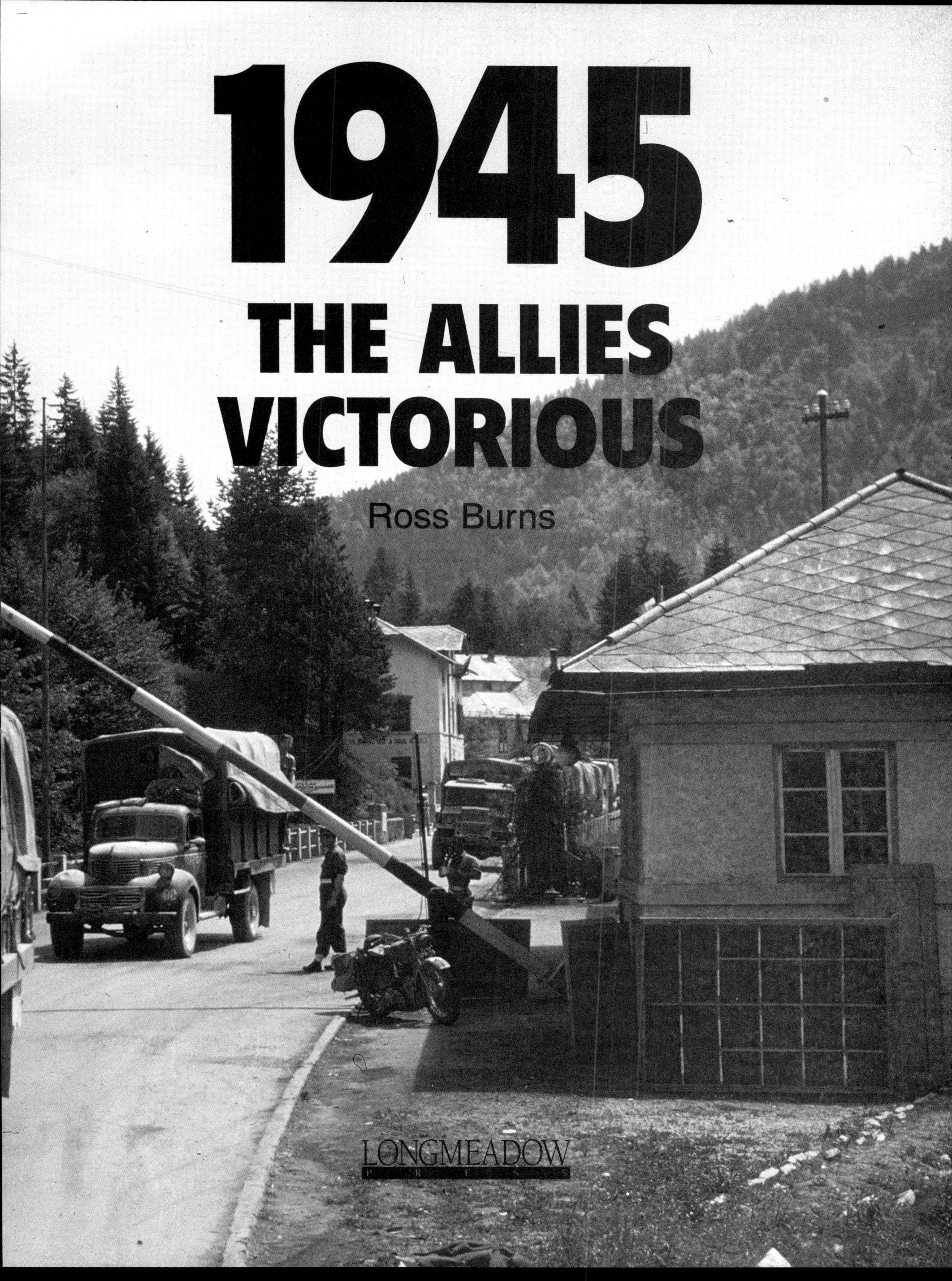

LONGMEADOW
PRESS

Published by Longmeadow Press, 201 High Ridge Road, Stamford, CT 06904.

ISBN 0-681-10341-8

Printed in China

First Longmeadow Press Edition

0 9 8 7 6 5 4 3 2 1

Page 1: Raising the US flag at Tenth Army headquarters, 22 June 1945.

Pages 2-3: Eighth Army trucks cross the Italian-Austrian border, May 1945.

These pages: A tank destroyer passes a disabled Panzer IV, Belgium, January 1945.

CONTENTS

1945 was the year in which the war was won.

Despite their recent brief setback in the Ardennes, the Western Allies began the year pushing steadily into Germany, would cross the Rhine in March and eventually link up with the Soviet forces at Torgau on the Elbe on 25 April. For their part the Soviets had rolled remorselessly across Poland and eastern Germany in the first months of the year before fighting their way into Berlin in a vicious battle in the second half of April.

Hitler continued to urge Germany to fight on, growing less and less in touch with reality day by day. He finally committed suicide on 30 April with the Soviet forces only yards from his bunker and his thousand year Reich did not long survive him. Britain and the US were able to celebrate V-E Day (Victory in Europe) on 8 May. We can now see that the reconquest of the two halves of Europe by armies espousing different political systems would govern two different approaches to the rebuilding of the continent's political and economic institutions but in May 1945 that, like the unfinished business of the punishment of war crimes and other matters, was a problem for the future.

In the Pacific the Allies continued to close in on Japan. All the time they were doing so they were also destroying Japan's capacity to make war by the very successful submarine campaign against her shipping and by the devastating bombing of her cities. In Burma the British inflicted a further series of major defeats on the Japanese and had recaptured the whole country by May. In the Philippines new landings were made on Luzon, the principal island of the group, in January and by March most of this island was in American hands also.

The US Marines captured the tiny stepping-stone island of Iwo Jima at great cost in February and the last stage before the planned invasion of the Japanese Home Islands was the bloody capture of Okinawa in April-June.

On 16 July 1945 a new element entered military and international affairs when the first atomic bomb was tested by the Americans at Alamagordo in New Mexico. President Truman (Roosevelt had died in April) decided that the atom bomb should be dropped on Japan in an attempt to end the war without the enormous Allied and Japanese casualties anticipated if the invasion of Japan itself was to be carried out. Hiroshima on 6 August and Nagasaki on the 9th were the targets for the two attacks. On 8 August Stalin kept his promise to the US and Britain from earlier in the war and declared war on Japan. Soviet forces were very quickly smashing through the Japanese in Manchuria. Whether because of these defeats or the atom bomb attacks has been debated ever since, but the Japanese quickly capitulated. World War II ended with the signing of the Japanese surrender aboard the USS *Missouri* in Tokyo Bay on 2 September 1945.

Right: A concentration camp inmate, rescued by the Allies, but perhaps too weak to survive. Such scenes rightly shocked the world.

Below left: US infantrymen fire on Japanese positions in the fiercely-defended Intramuros area of Manila in January 1945.

Below: Men of an RAF bomber squadron celebrate around one of their Lancaster aircraft.

Above: General Douglas MacArthur watches from a balcony window and a crowd of soldiers look on as a small group of Japanese soldiers surrender in Manila. MacArthur's promise, in the dark days of 1942, that he would return to the Philippines had been triumphantly fulfilled.

Left: Men of the 32nd Infantry Division in good heart at a soldiers' show on Luzon, the northernmost island of the Philippines in August 1945.

Top right: The US Army reoccupies Clark Field near Manila, as Japanese gun emplacements (background) sustain a direct hit.

Right: The final assault on Manila's last Japanese stronghold, the walled city of Intramuros, was delivered from the steps of the city's Post Office. Here men of the US 145th Infantry are seen in front of the Post Office building.

Above: Two platoons of American infantry fight their way along the Old Burma Road, reopened in January 1945 as the Japanese were pushed back in north Burma.

Left: Admiral Lord Louis Mountbatten, Supreme Allied Commander, Southeast Asia Theater, (left), visits General Douglas MacArthur, during his stopover in Manila, July 1945.

Top right: A scout car and a Sherman tank disembark from a makeshift barge on the Eastern bank of the Irrawaddy, February 1945, as the Allies advanced to engage the retreating Japanese forces.

Right: The outskirts of Pegu, 50 miles north of Rangoon, burn as the Fourteenth Army's Shermans roll southward to secure victory for General Sir William Slim.

202
202

Far left: An American landing craft damaged during the invasion of Iwo Jima.

Left: An airborne view of Iwo Jima from a 7th Air Force B-24 Liberator bomber, one of many sent to attack the strategically important – just eight square miles in size – island prior to the US landing.

Below: The soft, volcanic ash of the beach on Iwo Jima hampered the American landing effort, as the abandoned jeep clearly shows.

Right: Marine Corps personnel attend a briefing immediately prior to the Iwo Jima invasion.

Left: Vice-Admiral Richard Kelly Turner (left) with Major General Harry Schmidt and Lieutenant General Holland M Smith (right), the trio who directed operations against Iwo Jima.

Bottom left: Turner and Holland Smith survey the action at first hand.

Right: An observer on Iwo Jima locates an enemy machine gun emplacement on a map with a view to Allied artillery destroying it.

Below: The Second Battalion, 27th US Marines land on Iwo Jima, 19 February 1945. Two Marine divisions had landed by the time the Japanese opened their fire, hoping to make the invaders believe they would encounter no resistance but opening fire fatal minutes too late.

Top left: The smoke of battle obscures Mount Suribachi, the massif at the island's southernmost tip and the goal of the 5th Division, US Marine Corps as they work their way uphill from Red Beach . The mountain was secured after three costly days of combat.

Left: Marines with flamethrowers work their way towards Iwo Jima's Mount Suribachi. The US flag was raised on the summit on 23rd February, but major Japanese resistance on the island continued for a further three days.

Above: An aerial view of Iwo Jima, its airstrips (left and right) targeted by bombs of the 7th US Army Air Force. The cluster of bombs center hit gun emplacements.

Right: Despite withering Japanese small-arms fire, Marines establish a landline for field telephone communications with the front line.

Right: An amphibious tractor loaded with US Marines leaves an LST. Skill in amphibious operations was a key to US success in the inexorable advance towards the Japanese homeland.

Left: Marines blast Japanese positions near the base of Mount Suribachi. Landing on the south coast of the rocky island, US forces compressed the Japanese into the north-east corner where a network of underground defenses aided concealment.

Below: Marines go ashore at Iwo Jima. Hand-to-hand combat for control of the island cost the lives of nearly 7000 US servicemen: the 22,000 Japanese defenders were killed almost to a man.

Left: A lone American soldier stands watch over a group of German prisoners during the latter stages of the Battle of the Bulge.

Right: German graffiti, January 1945. The message reads: "Behind the last battle of this war stands our victory."

Far right: Wrapped up against the biting weather, a member of the 26th Division eats cold rations, 12 January 1945.

Below: An American column moves up to the front in the drive against the Bulge.

Winter der letzten Schlacht dieses Krieges
steht unser
Sieg

954 H 05
10

Left: An American DUKW 'waddles' into the Rhine for the crossing to the east bank. An ever increasing flow of men and material forges across the river, pouring into the rapidly expanding bridgehead.

Right: British soldiers advance with caution as their sector of the Allied front reached the Rhine in March 1945.

Below: In inhospitable winter conditions, American troops of the 9th Armored Division prepare to tow away Sherman tanks knocked out by the German drive near Bastogne, Belgium.

Left: Troops of a Scottish division leave their assault craft after crossing the Rhine. The drive from the Rhine to the Elbe was to meet pockets of determined German opposition.

Above: Two German soldiers captured by troops of the Third US Army on the outskirts of Margorette, Belgium, under military police guard.

Right: The capture, intact, of the Ludendorff rail bridge over the Rhine at Remagen by the US First Army on 7 March 1945 was the single most important Allied move in crossing the greatest water obstacle in Western Europe.

Below: British troops prepare boats and other bridging equipment for the Rhine crossings in their sector.

Left: US Sherman tanks push through Munich, April 1945, during the final days of the Third Reich.

Below: French troops make use of an improvised bridge to cross the River Lauter before entering the German village of Scheibonhard, March 1945.

Right: Members of the US 45th Division, Seventh Army, parade flags in Nuremberg's Luitpold Arena, April 1945.

Below right: Supported by a lone Sherman, infantry of the US 55th Armored Infantry Regiment run through the smoke-filled streets of Wernberg, Germany, April 1945.

Left: The Allied advance through Belgium into Germany was achieved in the face of not only the enemy but the weather. A British 17-pdr SP ploughs through the water on the Krahenburg Road.

Right: German high-ranking officers surrender at Field Marshal Montgomery's HQ on Luneberg Heath, 4 May 1945.

Far right: The German delegates have a conference among the trees.

Below: An American antiaircraft position on the banks of the Rhine.

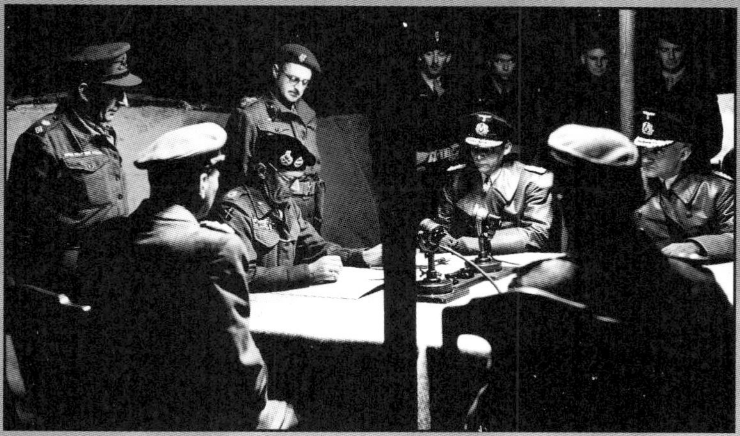

Top left: The American generals who helped pave the way to victory in Europe are pictured on 11 May 1945, four days after the formal cessation of hostilities, at 12th Army Group Headquarters, Bad Wildungen, Germany. Seated in the front row, left to right: General Simpson, US Ninth Army; General Patton, US Third Army; General Spaatz, USATAF; General Eisenhower, Supreme Allied Commander; General Bradley, 11th Army Group; General Hodges, US First Army and General Gerow, US Fifteenth Army.

Bottom left: The railway viaduct at Bielefeld photographed three days after the attack by RAF Bomber Command on 14th March 1945. The huge size of craters caused by 12,000lb and 22,000lb bombs can be seen when compared with the house at the bottom of the frame.

Right: SS troops under British guard load trucks with bodies from Belsen for transporting to burial grounds.

Below: The bodies of Mussolini, his mistress and other associates hang upside down after being shot by partisans in April 1945.

Top left: Nazi Field Marshal Gerd von Rundstedt, former German supreme commander on the Western Front, stands with his son, Leutnant Hans von Runstedt, and a German medical attendant (right) following his capture by troops of the 36th Division, Seventh US Army, at Bad Toelz, south of Munich, Germany. Von Rundstedt was receiving treatment for arthritis in a hospital in Bad Toelz when captured on 3 May. Put in charge of 'Fortress Europe' in the spring of 1944, von Rundstedt later led the retreat back into the Reich. Following the failure of the German Ardennes offensive, he was replaced by Field Marshal Kesselring in March 1945.

Above: The Soviet Guards Cavalry Corps meet units of the Third US Army on the Elbe, May 1945. Although it is likely the western Allies could have reached Berlin and Prague in the previous month, the US had pledged to the Soviets that the advance would stop at the Elbe.

Left: A street in the Karlsruhe area is renamed courtesy of a zealous American soldier, December 1944.

Right: A copy of the historic Unconditional Surrender Document signed by the German officers in Field Marshal Montgomery's tent. Note the change in the date, initialled by Montgomery.

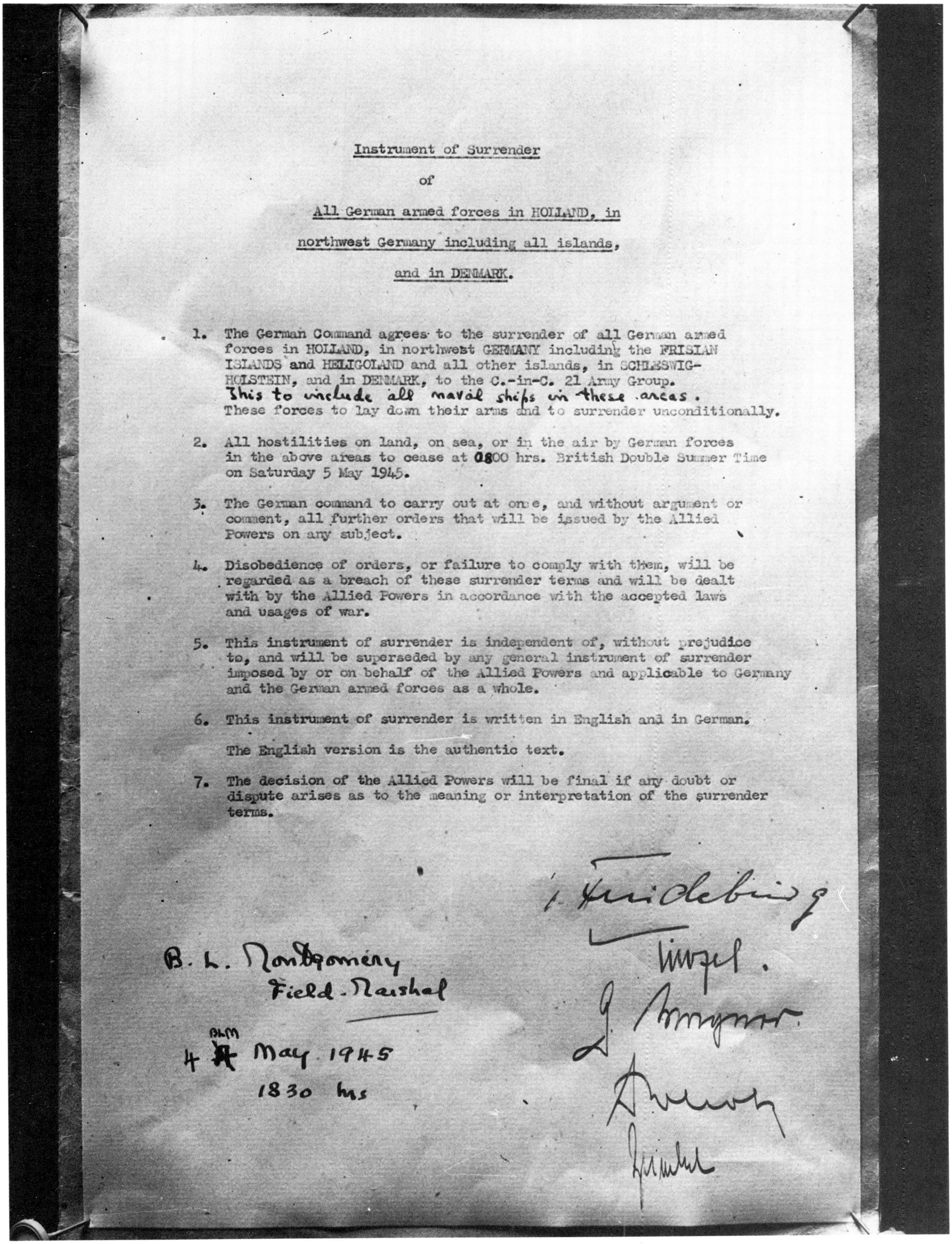

Instrument of Surrender

of

All German armed forces in HOLLAND, in

northwest Germany including all islands,

and in DENMARK.

1. The German Command agrees to the surrender of all German armed forces in HOLLAND, in northwest GERMANY including the FRISIAN ISLANDS and HELIGOLAND and all other islands, in SCHLESWIG-HOLSTEIN, and in DENMARK, to the C.-in-C. 21 Army Group. This to include all naval ships in these areas. These forces to lay down their arms and to surrender unconditionally.

2. All hostilities on land, on sea, or in the air by German forces in the above areas to cease at 0800 hrs. British Double Summer Time on Saturday 5 May 1945.

3. The German command to carry out at once, and without argument or comment, all further orders that will be issued by the Allied Powers on any subject.

4. Disobedience of orders, or failure to comply with them, will be regarded as a breach of these surrender terms and will be dealt with by the Allied Powers in accordance with the accepted laws and usages of war.

5. This instrument of surrender is independent of, without prejudice to, and will be superseded by any general instrument of surrender imposed by or on behalf of the Allied Powers and applicable to Germany and the German armed forces as a whole.

6. This instrument of surrender is written in English and in German.

The English version is the authentic text.

7. The decision of the Allied Powers will be final if any doubt or dispute arises as to the meaning or interpretation of the surrender terms.

B. L. Montgomery
Field-Marshal

4 May 1945
1830 hrs

Top left: The Soviet army enters Berlin in May 1945 after one of the hardest-fought battles of the war. The city would be partitioned for 45 years.

Above: Fighting rages in the Berlin streets as Soviet armor moves in from north and south to meet across the Charlottenberg Chaussee.

Left: Powerful Soviet artillery shells enemy fortifications, Berlin, 1945.

Below: Soviet troops cross the Oder River, the last major natural barrier between them and Berlin.

Above: 16 year old William Hübner, one of the youngest Iron Cross recipients. By 1945 boys even younger than this were being drafted into military service in Germany.

Left: A Waffen-SS soldier with anti-tank weapon travels to the front.

Right: The fall of Berlin in early May was never more graphically depicted than by this photograph of Soviet troops raising their flag over the last bastion of the Reich.

74
X
74
R
T 188888

Left: 10,000 men representing Britain's three fighting services march in triumph through the Charlottenberg Chaussee, 21 July 1945. Those present included Field Marshal Sir Henry Maitland-Wilson, Field Marshal Sir Harold Alexander, Admiral of the Fleet Sir Andrew Cunningham, Marshal of the Royal Air Force Sir Charles Portal, Field Marshal Sir Bernard Montgomery, Field Marshal Sir Alan Brooke and politicians Winston Churchill, Anthony Eden and Clement Attlee. Led by Brigadier J M K Spurling, DSO, the march past took 40 minutes to complete.

Bottom left: A battery of 'Katyusha' rocket mortars delivers a deadly salvo in the Carpathians, 1944.

Top right: An anti-tank missile is demonstrated to the German Home Guard in March 1945.

Right: A Wehrmacht armband identifies a member of the German Home Guard or Volksstürm.

Left: An Allied jeep enters the compound of one of Hitler's former headquarters after the German surrender.

Below: General Jodl signs the unconditional surrender document in Reims, 7 May 1945. Among the Allied war leaders present are Eisenhower's chief of staff, General Walter Bedell Smith, and General Carl Spaatz.

Right: The ceremony in Berlin on 9 May 1945 which saw the final ratification of the Third Reich's unconditional surrender terms. Top: Air Chief Marshal Sir Arthur Tedder looks on as the victor of the Battle of Berlin, Marshal Zhukov, examines the surrender terms. Bottom: Zhukov himself adds his signature to the surrender document.

Left: Some indication of the scale of the defeat inflicted on the armed forces of the Third Reich. These vehicles were surrendered to the US Army's 80th Infantry Division in Austria at the close of the war.

Below left: A photograph of Hamburg in May 1945 showing the devastating effect that the Allied strategic bombing campaign had on key industrial and economic targets.

Right: The surrender of Hitler's Kriegsmarine. These British vessels are moored at Copenhagen after a dash through the Skaggerak and Kattegat to reach the port and put German warships such as the *Prinz Eugen* and *Nürnberg* under their guns.

Below right: A familiar sight at the end of the conflict – German prisoners with a handful of Allied guards are sent to camps for processing and eventual release.

Right: Allied soldiers look through the war-ravaged state rooms of Hitler's Chancellery in Berlin.

Below: A Soviet parade marches down Unter den Linden in Berlin celebrating VE-Day.

Far right: The face of defeat. A weary veteran of the Battle of Berlin sits amid the rubble and ruins of the Reichstag.

Above: Marine F4U Corsair fighters are silhouetted against anti-aircraft tracers during a Japanese air raid on Yontan Airfield, Okinawa, in April 1945.

Left: Major General Lemuel C Shepherd, Jr, Commanding General of the 6th Marine Division, studies a map during the battle for Okinawa, April 1945.

Top right: Two US Marines armed with a Bazooka inch their way up a hill two miles north of the Okinawan capital, Naha.

Bottom right: The Japanese battleship *Yamato* is hit by a bomb during the Battle of Sibuyan Sea, 24 October 1944. The *Yamato* survived this engagement but was sunk by carrier planes during the Okinawa campaign. The *Yamato* was sent, effectively as a giant Kamikaze, to attack the US forces off Okinawa, without enough fuel aboard to make the return journey.

Left: One US Marine comforts another after witnessing the death of a comrade on an Okinawa hillside. These men took part in the bitter fighting waged against Shuri, the Japanese stronghold two miles east of Naha.

Below: US Marines deploy a 'Satchel' charge against a group of Japanese found in a cave. The destruction of the Japanese 32nd Army was achieved at an horrendous cost – over 8,000 men killed and nearly 32,000 wounded.

Top right: The carrier USS *Bunker Hill* (CV-17) sustains a hit. 36 US and British ships were lost at Okinawa, with hundreds more damaged.

Below right: The battleship USS *New Mexico* discharges her guns off Okinawa, April 1945. The invasion began on 1 April after a period of 'softening-up' with attacks from air and sea.

Below far right: A US Navy gun captain opening the breech of a 16-inch gun in a battleship's turret.

Left: The steeple of a Christian church below Shuri Castle on Okinawa provided a snipers' nest for the Japanese. The US Marines in the foreground are covering the building while a patrol comes in from the rear to neutralise it.

Bottom far left: A lone Marine stands in the wreckage of a theater building in Naha, May 1945.

Bottom left: A US Marine Corps photographer cleans the inside of the plexiglass nose of a P-38's belly tank, June 1945.

Right: The aftermath of a Kamikaze attack on HMS *Formidable*, stationed off Okinawa, on 4 May 1945. The British Pacific Fleet joined the main US forces for the Okinawa operations.

Below: US ships bombard Okinawa. The scale of losses sustained in the invasion lent weight to the argument for the use of the nuclear bomb to bring the war to a speedy conclusion.

Opposite left: One of USS *Alaska*'s Curtiss SC-1 float-planes moves up to the landing mat to be picked up by an aircraft crane. Air observation played an important part in tracking enemy ship movements.

Opposite right: Victory markings denoting Japanese planes downed are applied to a 5-inch gun director of a US destroyer.

Left: Vice-Admiral Marc Mitscher, commander of the US Task Force 58 that proved so successful in the Battle of the Philippine Sea.

Below: The radar picket destroyer *Aaron Ward* after being hit by five suicide planes during the Okinawa campaign. The radar picket ships operated some distance from the main Allied forces to give warning of attacks but often themselves became the Japanese targets.

MBS
CBS
NBC

Far left: Major General Curtis LeMay, who commanded the final stages of the strategic air operations against Japan.

Left: US President Harry Truman who, in July 1945, accepted his Chiefs of Staff's recommendation that Hiroshima – Japan's seventh largest city – should be the first target for the atomic bomb.

Bottom left: Boeing B-29s prepare to take off for Tokyo at one-minute intervals.

Top right: Incendiary bombs drop towards the dock area of Kobe, Japan's sixth largest city, as Marianas-based US B-29 Superfortresses drop 3000 tons of bombs and blast a ten-mile (16km) area extending along Osaka Bay, 4 June 1945.

Bottom right: Despite damage from anti-aircraft shell, a US B-29 Superfortress continues its bombing run over Osaka during an attack on Japan's largest industrial center on 1 June 1945.

Left: Soviet naval ratings of the Pacific Fleet hoist the Soviet flag over Port Arthur, 1945. The Soviets kept previous promises to join the war against Japan, declaring war on 8 August 1945. Their forces began an invasion of Manchuria the next day and some authorities believe that their rapid and overwhelming success did as much to make Japan surrender as the atom bomb attacks.

Below left: Colonel Paul Tibbetts with the B-29, named 'Enola Gay', he flew to bomb Hiroshima on 6 August 1945.

Below: Nagasaki was the second Japanese city to be subjected to atomic bomb attack, on 9 August 1945.

Top right and bottom right: The unparalleled destruction witnessed at Hiroshima and Nagasaki resulted in an estimated total of 131,000 immediate deaths plus many later and innumerable wounded.

Above: MacArthur signs the surrender document aboard the USS *Missouri* in Tokyo Bay on 2 September 1945, with Generals Wainwright and Percival watching. Both had just been freed from Japanese POW camps following their detention since respectively surrendering the Philippines and Malaya to the Japanese in 1942.

Above: High-ranking Allied officers board the USS *Missouri* for the formal signing ceremony that ended the war in the Far East.

Left: Lieutenant General Roy Geiger, Commanding General Fleet Marine Force, Pacific examines the card – signed by General MacArthur and Admirals Nimitz and Halsey – given to those who attended the surrender ceremony.

Right: The center of Hiroshima, Japan, obliterated by the first atomic bomb. The aiming point was the bridge, fourth from top in center. The harder, concrete structures were more resistant to the overpressure.

Bottom right: Japanese listen to news of the unconditional surrender, 15 August 1945. The decision was given in an unprecedented radio broadcast by Emperor Hirohito.

Left: The Royal Navy's *Duke of York*, decked out with the flags of the major Allied nations, rests at anchor in Tokyo Bay during the formal Japanese surrender ceremony.

Below left: Two wounded American servicemen watch the crowds from their balcony celebrating the Japanese capitulation and the end of World War II.

Below: General Douglas MacArthur steps down onto the runway of Ataugi airfield, near Tokyo, 30 August 1945.

Above right: General Tachibana prepares to sign the document that will ratify the surrender of the Bonin Islands to American forces, 3 September 1945.

Below right: MacArthur addresses a joint session of the Philippine Congress in Manila after its liberation.

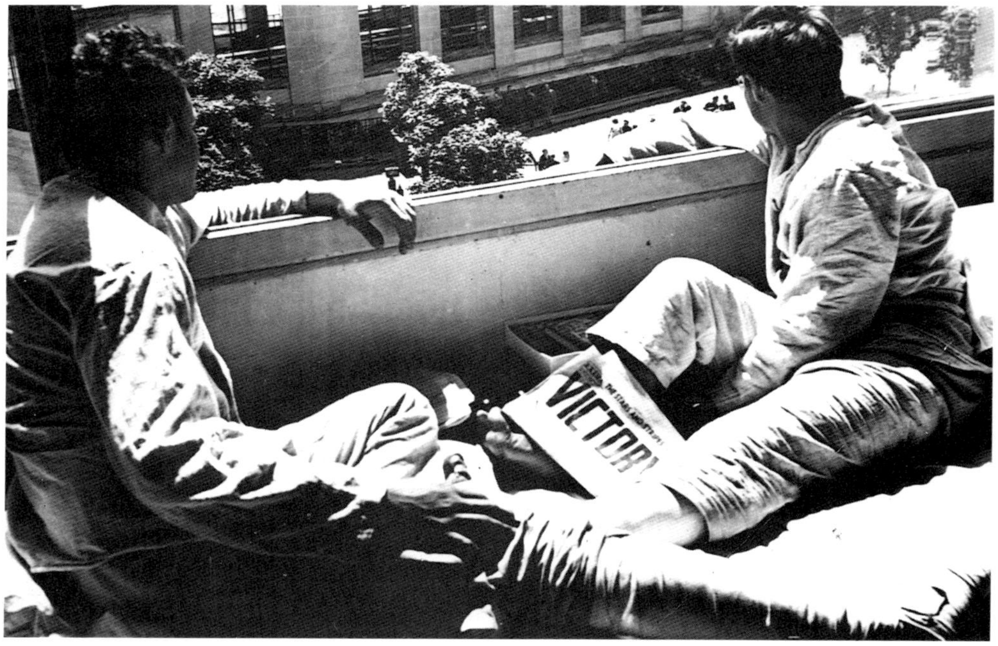

Left: A panoramic view of the Nuremberg Trials showing the accused and their legal representatives.

Below left: Members of the Nuremberg International Military Tribunal listen to the testimony of Czech surgeon Dr. Franz Blaha, who, as an inmate of Dachau, witnessed the Final Solution at first hand.

Right: Goering chats with Doenitz, while Hess, Ribbentrop and Keitel listen to the court during the first session of the war trials at Nuremberg's Palace of Justice, November 1945.

Below: The legacy of Hitler's "Thousand Year Reich" – Berlin 1945.

Acknowledgments

The publisher would like to thank David Eldred who designed this book. The following agencies provided photographic material:

Brompton Books Limited, pages 41(both), 44(bottom), 45.
Bundesarchiv, pages: 20(top), 21(top left), 36(both), 39(both).
Imperial War Museum, London, pages: 2-3, 7(both), 11(both), 20-21, 23, 24(top left), 24-25, 26(both), 27(both), 28-29(top three), 31(both), 33, 38(top), 40(top), 42-43(all four), 44(top), 51(top), 60(bottom left), 62-63(all four).
National Maritime Museum, London, page: 60(top).
Novosti Press Agency, pages: 34-35(all four), 37, 56(top).
U.S. Air Force, pages: 54-55(all five), 56(bottom two), 57(both).
U.S. Army, pages: 6, 8-9(all four), 10(both), 21(top right), 22, 22-23, 24(top right), 25(top), 27(bottom), 28-29, 30(top), 32(all three), 40(bottom), 59(both).
U.S. Marine Corps, pages: 1, 12-13(all four), 14-15(all four), 16-17(all four), 18-19(all three).
U.S. National Archives, pages: 61(top).
U.S. Navy, pages: 47(bottom), 48(all three), 51(bottom), 52-53(all four), 58(all three).
U.S. Signal Corps, pages: 4-5, 60(bottom right), 61(bottom).